TOO CUTE! BABY ANIMALS

Baby Ducks

by Colleen Sexton

Kaleidoscope
Minneapolis, MN

Where the Quest for Discovery Begins

This edition first published in 2024 by Kaleidoscope Publishing, Inc.

Kaleidoscope Publishing, Inc.
6012 Blue Circle Drive
Minnetonka, MN 55343

Library of Congress Control Number
2023936883

ISBN
978-1-64519-702-7 (library bound)
978-1-64519-750-8 (ebook)

Bigfoot Jr. lurks within one of the images in this book. It's up to you to find him!

Table of Contents

Just Hatched

A mother duck builds a nest. She lays eggs in the nest and sits on them to keep them warm.

Ducks build their nests near lakes, ponds, rivers, and oceans.

CRACK!
Baby ducks **hatch** from the eggs. They are called ducklings.

FUN FACT

There are more than 100 different kinds of ducks in the world.

The mother duck keeps her **brood** safe. The ducklings follow her wherever she goes.

Ducklings are loud! They quack and cheep to each other.

Fuzzy Ducklings

A young duckling is fuzzy. Tiny feathers called **down** keep it warm.

It flaps its two small wings.
But it cannot fly.

FUN FACT
Ducks bob their heads up and down when they are happy.

The duckling **waddles** on two legs.

The duckling splashes into a pond. It paddles its **webbed feet** to swim.

The duckling puts its head under the water to find food. It grabs a fish in its flat **bill**.

The duckling shakes its wet tail after it leaves the pond.

What Do Ducks Eat?

worms

bugs

plants

seeds

snails

fish

Parts of a Duckling

Duck Facts

Kind of Animal: bird

Eggs Laid: up to 15 at one time

Size When Hatched: about the size of a baseball

Home: near ponds, lakes, rivers, wetlands, and oceans

Feathered Fliers

The duckling gets bigger and bigger. Feathers grow on its body and wings.

The duckling learns to spread its wings and fly.

FUN FACT

Ducks use oil from near their tails to make their feathers waterproof.

The duckling grew up fast!

Most ducklings are fully grown about eight weeks after they hatch.

The duckling is now a young adult. It becomes a part of the **flock**.

The flock takes to the sky! The ducks fly far away to their warm home.

FUN FACT

Many ducks **migrate**. They live in one place in summer and travel to a warmer place in winter.

Photo Glossary

bill: a bird's beak or jaws

brood: a group of young animals cared for all at one time

down: the soft, fluffy feathers of ducklings and other baby birds

flock: a large group of birds that flies together

hatch: to break out of an egg

migrate: to move from one place to another; ducks migrate to warm places in winter.

waddles: moves side to side while taking short steps

waterproof: safe from water; something that is waterproof does not allow water to enter.

webbed feet: feet that have thin skin between the toes

Read More

Harris, Bizzy. *Ducks on the Farm*. Minneapolis, Minn.: Jump! Inc., 2021.

Myers, Maya. *Little Kids First Big Book of Baby Animals*. Washington, D.C.: National Geographic Kids, 2022.

Rathburn, Betsy. *Baby Ducks.* Minneapolis, Minn.: Bellwether Media, 2022.

Websites

FACTSURFER

Factsurfer.com gives you a safe, fun way to find more information.

1. Go to www.factsurfer.com.
2. Enter "Baby Ducks" into the search box and click 🔍
3. Select your book cover to see a list of related websites.

About the Author

Colleen Sexton is a writer and editor. She is the author of more than 100 nonfiction books for kids on topics ranging from astronauts to glaciers to elephants. She lives in Minnesota.

INDEX

PHOTO CREDITS

The images in this book are reproduced through the courtesy of: Natalia Vasylkivska/Shutterstock Images, cover; Goinyk Production/Shutterstock Images, title page, 15; iava777/Shutterstock Images, p. 3; IamSuperPear/Shutterstock Images, p. 4 (top); AEPhotographic/Shutterstock Images, p. 4 (bottom); Anneka/Shutterstock Images, p. 5 (circle); Ton Bangkeaw/Shutterstock Images, p. 5 (top); Olaf Holland/Shutterstock Images, p. 6–7 (top); Eric Isselee/Shutterstock Images, p. 6–7 (bottom); Volodymyr Burdiak/Shutterstock Images, p. 8; Eric Isselee/Shutterstock Images, p. 9; Matthew Williams-Ellis/Shutterstock Images, p. 10; Eric Isselee/Shutterstock Images, p. 11 (circle); dr.salama.photography/Shutterstock Images, p. 11; Shams F Amir/Shutterstock Images, p. 12; Mokhamad Bahrin/Shutterstock Images, p. 13 (top); Lovely Bird/Shutterstock Images, p. 13 (bugs); Lovely Bird/Shutterstock Images, p. 13 (fish); Brookgardener/Shutterstock Images, p. 13 (plants); JGade/Shutterstock Images, p. 13 (seeds); Aekawit Rammaket/Shutterstock Images, p. 13 (snails); Valentina Razumova/Shutterstock Images, p. 13 (worms); DenisNata/Shutterstock Images, p. 14; Stefan Rotter/Shutterstock Images, p. 16; Susan Hodgson/Shutterstock Images, p. 17; IamSuperPear/Shutterstock Images, p. 18 (top); Anneka/Shutterstock Images, p. 18 (bottom left); Africa Studio/Shutterstock Images, p. 18 (bottom right); DNTaylor Photography/Shutterstock Images, p. 19 (top); cynoclub/Shutterstock Images, p. 19 (bottom); schankz/Shutterstock Images, p. 20; Gallinago_media/Shutterstock Images, p. 20–21; taviphoto/Shutterstock Images, p. 22 (brood); Africa Studio/Shutterstock Images, p. 22 (bill); Valentina Proskurina/Shutterstock Images, p. 22 (down); Gallinago_media/Shutterstock Images, p. 22 (flock); Nataly Studio/Shutterstock Images, p. 22 (hatch); Gallinago_media/Shutterstock Images, p. 22 (migrate); New Africa/Shutterstock Images, p. 22 (waddles); Pascal Guay/Shutterstock Images, p. 22 (waterproof); DeawSS/Shutterstock Images, p. 22 (webbed feet); senk/Shutterstock Images, p. 23.